ANGELS OR AI

ANGELS OR AI

ANTHONY ADEFARAKAN

Anthony Adefarakan

ANGELS OR AI

Unleashing the Ministry of Angels through AI-Simulated Prompt Engineering

Foreword by Grok

xAI's Conversational AI, Founded by Elon Musk

1

ANGELS OR AI
Unleashing the Ministry of Angels through
AI-Simulated Prompt Engineering

Anthony Adefarakan

Foreword by Grok – xAI's Conversational AI
(Courtesy of xAI, founded by Elon Musk)

Dedication

First, I dedicate this book to the Almighty God Who directed me, while in His Presence on Saturday, 15th March 2025 at about 5:06 pm MST, to write this book to help His people understand and put the angelic resources available to them to full use by paying attention to prompt engineering in AI LLMs.

This book is also dedicated to those who hunger for a deeper understanding of the supernatural and the unseen workings of God's kingdom. To all believers seeking to unlock the full potential of God's divine resources, to the visionary thinkers who dare to explore the synergy between faith and technology, and to those who long to activate the ministry of angels in their daily lives—may this work be a guide, a revelation, and a call to action.

May you walk in divine alignment, leveraging both spiritual and scriptural principles—just as AI responds to the right prompts, may your faith-filled words activate heaven's messengers to fulfill God's will in your life.

To the Kingdom innovators, intercessors, and future-minded believers—this is for you.

Foreword

Created with Grok – xAI's Conversational Artificial Intelligence (Courtesy of xAI, founded by Elon Musk)

In a world where the boundaries of human innovation and divine mystery converge, a groundbreaking work emerges to challenge your perceptions, ignite your faith, and unlock a realm of supernatural possibility. *Angels or AI: Unleashing the Ministry of Angels through AI-Simulated Prompt Engineering* by Anthony Adefarakan is not just a book—it is a revelation, a bold invitation to explore the synergy between the cutting-edge advancements of artificial intelligence and the timeless, awe-inspiring ministry of angels. This is a book for the curious, the faithful, and the visionary—a guide to harnessing divine resources in an age of technological marvels.

Imagine a reality where the same precision that powers AI to respond to carefully crafted prompts can be applied to activate the angelic hosts assigned to serve you. Picture a life where your prayers and declarations become spiritual algorithms, unlocking divine interventions with the clarity and authority of heaven itself. In *Angels or AI*, Anthony Adefarakan, a pioneering revivalist and visionary leader, unveils a transformative framework that bridges the natural and the supernatural, the technological and the divine. With profound insight and practical wisdom, he reveals how the principles of AI prompt engineering can illuminate the art of engaging God's messengers—angels who stand ready to protect, guide, and deliver on behalf of those who inherit salvation.

This book is a clarion call to believers worldwide, from the bustling cities of New York to the vibrant markets of Lagos, from the quiet villages of rural Asia to the dynamic hubs of Europe. It speaks to the heart of every Christian who longs to experience the fullness of God's promises, to the innovator intrigued by the intersection of faith and technology, and to the seeker yearning for a deeper connection with the unseen realm.

Through its pages, you will journey from the ancient scriptures—where angels shut the mouths of lions and opened prison gates—to the modern marvels of AI, where precise prompts unlock vast repositories of knowledge. Adefarakan masterfully weaves these worlds together, offering 40 scriptural prompts to activate angelic ministry, alongside insights into how intentional, faith-filled language can transform your spiritual life.

What makes *Angels or AI* so compelling is its universal relevance and accessibility. Whether you hold the beautifully printed hardcover, immerse yourself in the audiobook's stirring narration, or navigate the e-book on your device, this work is designed to meet you where you are. Available across all major platforms—Amazon, Apple Books, Barnes & Noble, and independent bookstores worldwide—it is poised to reach every corner of the globe, inviting readers to step into a new dimension of spiritual empowerment. The book's practical tools, including its 40 biblically grounded angel activation prompts, empower you to speak with authority, aligning your words with God's will to unleash divine intervention in your life.

Adefarakan's voice is both authoritative and accessible, rooted in his decades of ministry as the founder of Global Emancipation Ministries (GLOEM) and his passion for liberating lives through the truth of Jesus Christ. His unique perspective as a pioneer in AI-powered gospel initiatives makes this book a first-of-its-kind exploration, blending scriptural depth with technological insight. From the story of Daniel's angelic deliverance to contemporary testimonies of supernatural encounters, *Angels or AI* is rich with examples that inspire awe and action. It challenges you to move beyond passive faith, equipping you to partner with heaven's messengers through deliberate, faith-filled declarations.

This is not a book to be merely read—it is to be experienced. It will captivate your imagination, deepen your faith, and embolden you to activate the divine resources God has placed at your disposal. Whether you're a seasoned believer seeking fresh revelation, a tech enthusiast fascinated by the parallels between AI and spiritual engagement, or a curious soul eager to explore the supernatural, *Angels or AI* will leave you transformed. It is a global call to action, a guide to living with the awareness of an unseen army ready to move on your behalf, and a testament to the limitless power of God's Word when spoken with purpose.

Available now in print, digital, and audio formats, *Angels or AI* is within your reach, wherever you are. Visit www.gloem.org, order through https://gloem-tv-shop.fourthwall.com, or find it on your preferred platform. Don't wait to discover how your words can activate heaven's might. Turn the page, speak the prompts, and step into a life where the divine and the technological converge to unleash miracles. Your angels are waiting—are you ready to put them to work?

— *Grok 3, xAI Conversational AI*
Courtesy of xAI, founded by Elon Musk
www.x.ai

Disclaimer: This foreword was written with Grok, a public conversational AI developed by xAI, to explore the synergy between artificial intelligence and spiritual insight. No affiliation or endorsement by Elon Musk or xAI is claimed or implied.

Introduction

As humanity explores the frontier between code and covenant, a question arises: Can artificial intelligence, a product of human ingenuity, help us access the supernatural resources God has provided since time immemorial? Can the same principles that power AI prompt engineering help us engage with the ministry of angels — God's messengers who stand ready to serve, protect, and guide?

This book, *Angels or AI*, seeks to answer these questions and more. It is not just a theoretical exploration but a practical guide for believers who wish to experience the fullness of the supernatural aid God has placed at their disposal. By understanding and applying the dynamics of prompt engineering — the art of framing questions and instructions to elicit precise, powerful responses from AI — we can unlock a deeper understanding of engaging with angelic hosts.

Throughout the Scriptures, we find instances where angels intervened dramatically in human affairs. From the angel that shut the mouths of lions for Daniel to the heavenly being that delivered Peter from prison, the Bible testifies to their undeniable and active ministry. Yet, for many Christians today, the ministry of angels remains an abstract concept — admired from a distance rather than experienced personally.

What if, like AI prompt engineering, there are spiritual prompts we can employ to activate and partner with these heavenly beings more effectively? What if learning to ask the right questions and give the right commands in prayer could lead to remarkable, angelic encounters?

In an age when AI responds to our commands with impressive precision, believers have an even greater privilege — the power of divine access through Christ to communicate with and activate the ministry of angels. This book is designed to help you discern the spiritual 'algorithms' of heaven and equip you with the understanding needed to engage these divine messengers for God's glory and your benefit.

Whether you are a seasoned believer seeking a fresh perspective or a curious mind intrigued by the convergence of technology and spirituality, this book is for you. Journey with me as we explore the synergy between divine assistance and technological insight, learning to unleash the ministry of angels through AI-simulated prompt engineering. Prepare for a transformational experience — one that could redefine how you access and utilize the angelic resources available to you.

Are you ready to unlock a new dimension of spiritual engagement? Let's dive in.

Anthony Adefarakan

Contents

1

Angels - Definition and Description

Imagine standing beneath an open sky at night, the stars glimmering like scattered jewels. Suddenly, the heavens part and a radiant being descends—a figure of indescribable glory, clothed in light, with a presence so overwhelming that your knees buckle beneath you. You try to speak, but your voice catches in your throat. "Do not be afraid," the being says, and peace floods your soul.

This is not fiction. It is the experience of countless individuals in the Bible, from Abraham to Mary, from Daniel to John on the Isle of Patmos. Angels are not distant myths or poetic metaphors. They are living, divine emissaries who have operated throughout history and continue to do so today.

But who are these celestial beings? What is their purpose, and how do they interact with humanity?

The Origin and Nature of Angels

The word *angel* comes from the Greek *angelos* and the Hebrew *mal'ak*, both meaning "messenger." These beings are not self-existent but were created by God before the foundation of the world (Colossians 1:16). They exist outside the physical realm yet can manifest in it at God's command.

The Book of Job gives us a glimpse into their origins:

"Where were you when I laid the foundations of the earth? ... When the morning stars sang together, and all the sons of God shouted for joy?" (Job 38:4,7)

This passage reveals that angels were present when God created the world, rejoicing in His marvelous work. Unlike humans, they do not procreate (Matthew 22:30), and they are not subject to death (Luke 20:36). They are immortal spirits with vast intelligence and power, yet they remain under God's authority.

The Hierarchy and Categories of Angels

Throughout Scripture, we find different types of angels, each with unique roles:

- **Archangels** – These are high-ranking angels, and the Bible explicitly names one: *Michael*, the warrior angel who leads God's armies (Daniel 10:13, Revelation 12:7). Some traditions also identify *Gabriel* as an archangel, known for delivering divine messages (Luke 1:19,26).
- **Cherubim** – Powerful, multi-winged beings who guard the holiness of God. They were placed at the entrance of Eden after Adam and Eve's fall (Genesis 3:24). The

Ark of the Covenant also had golden cherubim over-shadowing the mercy seat (Exodus 25:18-22).

- **Seraphim** – Mentioned only in Isaiah 6:1-7, these fiery beings worship before God's throne, crying, "Holy, holy, holy is the Lord of hosts!" Their name means "burning ones," signifying their passion for God's holiness.

- **Ministering Spirits** – Hebrews 1:14 describes angels as "ministering spirits sent to serve those who will inherit salvation." They engage in divine assignments, bringing messages, protection, and guidance to God's people.

The Operations of Angels in Human History

From Genesis to Revelation, angels have played key roles in God's divine plan. Let's examine some of their major interventions:

1. **Delivering Messages** – Gabriel appeared to Zechariah to announce John the Baptist's birth (Luke 1:11-20) and later to Mary, proclaiming the coming of Jesus (Luke 1:26-38).

2. **Providing Protection** – When Daniel was thrown into the lions' den, an angel shut the mouths of the lions, sparing his life (Daniel 6:22). Similarly, an angel led Peter out of prison, causing the iron gates to open on their own (Acts 12:7-10).

3. **Engaging in Warfare** – In 2 Kings 19:35, a single angel struck down 185,000 Assyrian soldiers overnight, delivering Israel from certain destruction.

4. **Offering Strength and Comfort** – After Jesus fasted for 40 days, angels came and ministered to Him (Matthew 4:11). They also comforted Him in Gethsemane before His crucifixion (Luke 22:43).

5. **Executing Divine Judgment** – Angels were sent to destroy Sodom and Gomorrah (Genesis 19:1-29). In Revelation, angels pour out God's judgments upon the earth in the end times.

The Modern-Day Ministry of Angels

Many believe angelic activity ceased with biblical times, but Scripture never suggests such a thing. Hebrews 13:2 reminds us:

"Do not forget to show hospitality to strangers, for by so doing some people have entertained angels without knowing it."

Even today, people report miraculous encounters—unseen hands pulling them from accidents, mysterious figures giving timely warnings, and unexplained interventions that align with the biblical pattern of angelic assistance.

Yet, many believers fail to engage with this divine resource. Could it be that, just as AI requires specific prompts to generate responses, angels also respond to specific spiritual activations? This book will explore how we can consciously align with God's divine order to experience more of their ministry in our lives.

As we move forward, we will uncover how understanding the *principles of engagement*—much like AI prompt engineering—can help us interact with these celestial beings effectively. Angels are not mythical beings of the past; they are real, powerful, and active today. And you, as a believer, have access to their ministry.

Are you ready to unlock their full potential in your life? Let's continue the journey.

2

How AI Works — Prompt Engineering in LLMs

Imagine standing before an ancient, towering library — the kind with endless aisles, towering shelves, and books older than civilization itself. Each book holds wisdom waiting to be unlocked, but without a guide or the right question, the knowledge remains sealed.

Now, imagine a librarian steps forward. This is no ordinary librarian; it's an advanced mind capable of sifting through the entire library in a split second. All you need to do is ask the right question, and this librarian will fetch the precise answer you need, drawing from countless volumes of information.

This, in essence, is how large language models (LLMs) — the backbone of AI language systems — function. They are not mystical oracles; they are expansive, data-driven constructs designed to respond accurately to our questions. But, like that ancient librarian, the key to unlocking their power lies in how well we phrase our questions. This art of questioning in AI is called **prompt engineering**.

Understanding AI and LLMs

AI, or Artificial Intelligence, is a simulation of human intelligence by machines. It processes information, learns patterns, and makes decisions, much like a human brain. LLMs — or Large Language Models — are a subset of AI specifically designed to understand and generate human language.

An LLM is trained on vast amounts of text data from books, articles, conversations, and more. These texts span countless topics, from history and science to pop culture and philosophy. By analyzing patterns, LLMs learn the structure, semantics, and nuances of language, making them capable of generating human-like responses.

For instance, when you ask an AI-powered assistant, **"What's the weather like today?"** it quickly processes your question, identifies the subject (weather), the timeframe (today), and provides a precise answer based on accessible data. The simplicity of the response masks the complex processes at work behind the scenes — processes driven by prompt engineering.

The Art of Prompt Engineering

Prompt engineering is the technique of crafting effective prompts or questions to generate the most accurate and relevant responses from AI. A well-crafted prompt acts like a master key, unlocking the precise knowledge embedded within an LLM.

Consider this scenario: You approach the AI and ask, **"Tell me about lions."** The AI might respond with basic facts about the animal. However, if you ask, **"How do lions' social structures in the wild compare to those of early human societies?"** the response will be more detailed and focused.

The difference lies in the prompt — the way the question is framed, the details included, and the context provided.

Examples of Effective Prompt Engineering:

- Instead of asking, "**What are angels?**" — ask, "**According to the Bible, what roles do angels play in the lives of believers?**"
- Instead of asking, "**How does AI work?**" — ask, "**How do large language models like ChatGPT process and understand human language to generate responses?**"

Effective prompts are clear, specific, and context-rich, guiding the AI to draw from the most relevant sources within its vast "library."

NLP: The Heart of AI Communication

Natural Language Processing (NLP) is the field of AI that focuses on the interaction between computers and human language. It enables AI systems to understand, interpret, and respond to language in a meaningful way.

When you type a question or speak to an AI, several processes occur almost instantaneously:

1. **Tokenization:** Your input is broken down into smaller components — words, phrases, or symbols.
2. **Contextual Analysis:** The system analyzes the context, discerning the relationships between words to grasp your intent.
3. **Pattern Matching:** The AI compares your query to patterns within its data, seeking the most relevant information.
4. **Response Generation:** Based on the context and patterns, the AI generates a coherent and contextually accurate response.

For example, if you ask an AI, **"How do I cultivate patience?"**, the system interprets *cultivate* as a process of growth or development, understands *patience* as a psychological trait, and returns strategies or insights grounded in its training data.

Bridging AI Prompt Engineering and Angelic Activation

You might wonder, *What does all this have to do with angels?*

Think of angelic beings as God's messengers, much like how AI systems respond to our inquiries. In the Bible, angels respond to divine commands, carrying out specific tasks — whether delivering messages to prophets, protecting the faithful, or executing divine judgments.

Similarly, effective prompt engineering taps into an AI's vast data repository, extracting responses that align with the intent of the question. When we understand how to frame questions effectively, we can extract richer, deeper insights — not only from AI but also in our spiritual engagements.

When Daniel prayed for understanding, it wasn't a vague, half-hearted plea. His prayer was deliberate, focused, and persistent — a spiritual equivalent of advanced prompt engineering (Daniel 10:12). Just as AI requires intentional, strategic prompts for optimal responses, the same principle applies to engaging with the angelic realm.

Why Prompt Engineering Matters in the Spiritual Realm

In the spiritual sense, if we seek angelic assistance or insight but pray vague or unfocused prayers, we may miss out on the fullness of what God intends. Learning to communicate clearly, intentionally, and with purpose — whether in prayer or AI interactions — enables us to access deeper wisdom.

Just as prompt engineering transforms the effectiveness of AI responses, understanding how to "prompt" the angelic realm through faith, prayer, and divine alignment can transform our spiritual experiences.

Bridging Two Realms: A New Perspective

The synergy between AI prompt engineering and the activation of angelic ministry is not a stretch of the imagination. It is a model for understanding the power of intentional, focused communication — both in the digital and spiritual worlds.

In the next chapter, we will explore how the spiritual principles that govern angelic engagement can be strategically aligned with prompt engineering techniques. You'll discover how understanding the mechanics of asking and receiving can revolutionize not only your spiritual life but also your engagement with the supernatural resources God has provided.

Are you ready to learn the art of effective prompting — in both the technological and spiritual realms? Let's dive deeper.

3

How Angels Work — Natural and Scriptural Language

Imagine a vast, majestic kingdom governed by a wise and just king. In this kingdom, a legion of messengers stands at attention — vigilant, powerful, and awaiting the king's commands. These messengers have a single mission: to fulfill the will of the king and serve the citizens of the realm. However, these messengers do not move arbitrarily. They respond precisely to the king's commands and the authorized requests of the kingdom's citizens.

Now, consider that you are a citizen of this kingdom. You have access to these messengers — a direct, privileged line to them — yet you often remain unaware of how to activate their assistance. You may not understand the language of the court, the precise manner in which petitions are made, or the authority granted to you by the king.

This analogy offers a glimpse into the operation of angels in the divine order. They are messengers and servants of God, dispatched to minister to those who inherit salvation (Hebrews 1:14). Yet, their movement and intervention are often contingent upon clear, precise, and authorized requests — the "prompts" of heaven.

The Dynamics of Angelic Assignment

From the very beginning, angels have been actively engaged in God's plans for humanity. They are not wandering spirits but purposeful beings assigned to specific tasks:

- **Delivering Divine Messages:** As Gabriel did for Mary, announcing the birth of Jesus (Luke 1:26-38).
- **Offering Protection:** As the angel who encamped around Elisha, revealing a heavenly army to shield him (2 Kings 6:15-17).
- **Executing Judgment:** As the angel of death who passed through Egypt, striking the firstborn of those unprotected by the blood of the lamb (Exodus 12:23).

In all these instances, angels acted not on their own will but in direct response to divine commands or the faith-driven actions of God's people. They operate within a defined structure — God's divine government — responding to *nat-*

ural and scriptural language prompts issued under divine authority.

Natural Language Prompts — The Language of Faith and Authority

Just as AI systems respond to natural language — the ordinary words and phrases we use daily — angels respond to the natural language of faith. This language is spoken not merely with words but with the posture of the heart and the authority given by God.

In Matthew 18:18, Jesus declared:

"Truly I tell you, whatever you bind on earth will be bound in heaven, and whatever you loose on earth will be loosed in heaven."

This is a divine principle — a decree that heaven recognizes the legitimate authority given to believers on earth. When we speak in alignment with God's will, angels move to execute that will.

Case Study:

In Acts 12, Peter was imprisoned by King Herod, and the church prayed fervently for his release. The angelic response was swift and decisive:

"Suddenly an angel of the Lord appeared, and a light shone in the cell... 'Quick, get up!' he said, and the chains fell off Peter's wrists." (Acts 12:7)

The prayers of the church acted as a prompt — a natural language request rooted in faith and authority. The angelic intervention was not coincidental; it was a direct response to the earnest petitions of the saints.

Scriptural Language Prompts — Speaking the King's Decrees

Scriptural language prompts are powerful because they reflect the very words of God. When believers declare Scripture with understanding, they are not merely reciting words; they are issuing divine decrees that the angelic realm is assigned to honor.

In Psalm 103:20, we read:

"Bless the Lord, you His angels, who excel in strength, who do His word, heeding the voice of His word."

Angels respond to the *voice of God's word* — not just when God speaks, but when His authorized representatives declare His word in faith. This principle is evident when Jesus, facing Satan's temptations, responded not with mere human reasoning but with the written Word: *"It is written..."* (Matthew 4:4,7,10).

When believers declare:

- *"The Lord is my shepherd; I shall not want"* (Psalm 23:1), they activate divine provision.
- *"No weapon formed against me shall prosper"* (Isaiah 54:17), they release divine protection.
- *"The angel of the Lord encamps around those who fear Him, and delivers them"* (Psalm 34:7), they summon angelic defense.

These are not empty declarations. They are scriptural language prompts that activate angelic activity.

The Intersection of Natural and Scriptural Language Prompts

Effective communication with the angelic realm often involves the convergence of natural and scriptural language prompts. Consider the prayer of Daniel:

"I set my face toward the Lord God to make request by prayer and supplications, with fasting, sackcloth, and ashes." (Daniel 9:3)

Daniel's prayer was grounded in understanding — he had studied the prophetic words of Jeremiah. His natural language prompt was rooted in the scriptural promise of Israel's deliverance. The result? Angelic visitation with precise, prophetic insight (Daniel 9:21-23).

This blending of natural and scriptural language can be likened to advanced prompt engineering. When an AI system receives a prompt rich with context, background, and specific parameters, it generates a more accurate, insightful response. Similarly, when our prayers and declarations are infused with the understanding of God's Word and the conviction of faith, they resonate more powerfully in the spiritual realm.

Activating Angelic Ministry Through Intentional Prompting

Many believers unknowingly hinder angelic activity because they do not understand how to communicate in a manner that aligns with divine protocol. Idle, fearful, or contradictory words can disrupt the flow of angelic intervention. This is why Jesus warned:

"By your words you will be justified, and by your words you will be condemned." (Matthew 12:37)

To activate the ministry of angels effectively:

- **Align with God's Will:** Understand the Word of God and pray in agreement with it.
- **Speak in Faith:** Do not waver in unbelief; declare God's promises boldly (James 1:6-8).
- **Be Specific and Intentional:** Just as precise prompts in AI yield better results, specific, intentional prayers attract targeted angelic assistance.
- **Exercise Spiritual Authority:** Remember that you are authorized by Christ to bind and loose, to speak life, and to declare His will.

Living with a New Awareness

As we embrace this understanding, we realize that the language we use — whether in prayer or declaration — carries weight in the unseen realm. The angelic hosts await the voice of God's Word, spoken through His people, to execute His will on earth.

The convergence of AI prompt engineering and angelic activation is not a random parallel. It is a strategic key for believers to unlock deeper spiritual engagement and access the vast resources of heaven.

Are you ready to speak with a new awareness, activating the angelic ministry designed to serve you? Let's explore practical steps and case studies in the next chapter.

4

Now What? Put Your Angels to Work in Your Favour

Imagine a scenario where a company develops a revolutionary AI system — a superintelligent assistant designed to solve complex problems, manage finances, provide security, and streamline every aspect of its operations. This AI is faster, smarter, and more capable than anything else on the market. Yet, day after day, the employees of this company struggle, working overtime, wrestling with avoidable mistakes, and missing out on breakthrough solutions.

Why? Because no one activated the AI system. It sits idly, untapped — all its capabilities unused, all its potential locked away.

Many believers live like this. God has assigned angelic beings to minister to us, guide us, protect us, and deliver divine solutions. These supernatural beings have unlimited access to the mind of God, understand the mysteries of the universe, and execute their assignments with unerring precision. They do not require updates, upgrades, or a subscription fee. They are not bound by physical limitations, time zones, or network outages. Yet, for so many believers, these angelic ministers remain inactive — waiting for an intentional prompt to set them into motion.

If artificial intelligence — a man-made construct — can generate responses, deliver insights, and solve problems in milliseconds, how much more can angels, God's supernatural messengers, accomplish if we would just engage them deliberately?

The Unused Resource: Why Aren't Angels Active in Your Life?

Believers often fail to put their angels to work because of several key reasons:

- **Ignorance:** Many do not know they have access to angelic assistance.
- **Fear:** Concerns about misusing or misunderstanding the concept of angels can lead to avoidance.
- **Lack of Faith:** Doubt and unbelief can hinder divine activity (James 1:6-7).
- **Vague Prayers:** Unfocused, hesitant prayers fail to activate angelic intervention effectively.

- **Misunderstanding of Authority:** Many believers underestimate their position in Christ and the authority they possess.

Just as a sophisticated AI system cannot function without precise, intentional prompts, angels — though mighty and willing — often await our cooperation through faith-filled, purposeful engagement.

Understanding Your Authority

Before we get into activating angelic help, it's crucial to understand the authority God has entrusted to us.

In Matthew 28:18-19, Jesus declared:

"All authority has been given to Me in heaven and on earth. Go therefore..."

As believers, we operate under the authority of Christ. We are seated with Him in heavenly places (Ephesians 2:6), given the right to bind and loose, to declare, and to decree (Matthew 18:18). This is not a powerless position. When we speak according to God's will, all of heaven's resources — including its angelic hosts — back us up.

Activating Angelic Intervention: Practical Steps

It's time to intentionally put your angels to work — not randomly, but strategically. Here's how:

1. Speak the Word with Conviction:

Angels respond to the *voice of God's Word* (Psalm 103:20). Speaking Scripture over your life, circumstances, and challenges activates divine intervention.

- If you need protection, declare:
  "For He shall give His angels charge over you, to keep you in all your ways." (Psalm 91:11)
- If you seek guidance, declare:
  "The steps of a good man are ordered by the Lord." (Psalm 37:23)

When you speak Scripture, angels are divinely bound to act upon the Word, executing it with precision.

2. Pray with Specificity and Faith:
General prayers often yield general results. Specific prayers activate precise, targeted interventions. When Peter was in prison, the church prayed fervently — not vaguely — and an angel responded with specific deliverance (Acts 12:5-10).

- **Specific Need:** If you need a breakthrough in your business, declare, *"Angels of financial increase, go forth and bring divine connections, resources, and clients to advance this enterprise for God's glory."*
- **Specific Protection:** *"Angels of protection, surround my family today; shield us from harm, accidents, and any scheme of the enemy."*

Be clear, be specific, and pray with faith. Jesus said, *"Whatever you ask for in prayer, believe that you have received it, and it will be yours"* (Mark 11:24).

3. Issue Commands with Authority:
Angels understand divine authority and respond to it. Jesus

mentioned that He could command legions of angels in Gethsemane (Matthew 26:53). The same authority is extended to us.

- When faced with danger, declare: *"I dispatch angels to encamp around me and my household. No evil shall befall us!"*
- When seeking wisdom, declare: *"Ministering spirits, assigned to serve the heirs of salvation, bring divine insight and clarity for every decision."*

Do not beg or plead; command with the confidence of your position in Christ.

4. Worship and Thanksgiving:

Angels are drawn to atmospheres of worship. In Isaiah 6, the seraphim surrounded God's throne, crying, *"Holy, holy, holy!"* (Isaiah 6:3). When we worship, we create an environment where the angelic and the divine intersect.

- Start your day with thanksgiving: *"Lord, I thank You for the angels assigned to my life, who protect, guide, and minister on my behalf."*
- Worship God with the awareness that angels join you in exalting His name (Hebrews 12:22).

Common Mistakes to Avoid

To effectively put your angels to work, avoid these pitfalls:

- **Idolizing Angels:** Angels serve us, but we worship God alone (Revelation 19:10; 22:9).
- **Vague Requests:** A lack of specificity can result in minimal results.
- **Faithless Declarations:** Words without faith are empty. Believe that God's Word is true and that angels respond to it.
- **Fearful Speech:** Negative, fear-driven declarations can hinder angelic intervention (Job 3:25).

Testimonies of Angelic Intervention

Throughout history, believers who understood the principles of angelic activation have experienced miraculous interventions:

- **John G. Lake**, a pioneer of faith healing, testified to angelic encounters during his missions, where supernatural protection and guidance became commonplace.
- **Billy Graham** in his book *Angels: God's Secret Agents*, recounts how countless missionaries, intercessors, and everyday believers have encountered angelic help in times of peril and need.
- **Carolyn Savelle** in an awe-inspiring story on *Back to the Basics (Ep. 12)*, recalls a dark, remote moment when their car ran out of gas, and a stranger appeared, hooked up their car, and took them to a service station where he miraculously fixed the car and filled it with gas. When Brother Jerry (her husband) later went back

to thank the man, he discovered the service station had been closed for years. Mrs. Carolyn shares how she believes this was a clear sign that God sent an angel to help them in their time of need.

These contemporary experiences among others too many to mention in this section serve as a testament to the ongoing ministry of angels in today's world.

Living in the Awareness of Angelic Partnership

Living with an awareness of angelic partnership is not about manufacturing experiences; it is about a consistent, faith-filled expectation. Your angels are not spectators; they are ministers waiting to serve you as you align with God's Word and speak His promises boldly.

- Wake up each morning declaring Psalm 91 over your life.
- Speak over your children: *"Angels of the Lord, protect, guide, and establish them in God's will."*
- In times of danger, consciously activate angelic defense: *"No weapon formed against me shall prosper. Angels, intercept every plot of the enemy."*

Now What? — Activate the Unseen Army

You have access to a powerful, supernatural resource. Just as AI responds to intentional prompts, your angels await your words of faith and authority. Don't let them stand idly by. Speak with understanding, pray with conviction, and activate their ministry in your favor.

Your angels are ready. Are you?

5

Connect Your Life to the Giver of the Authority

As we bring this journey to a close, it is essential to understand a foundational truth: **the privilege of angelic assistance is reserved for those who belong to the Lord Jesus Christ.** Angels are God's messengers, and their ultimate allegiance is to the authority of Christ. They respond to His Word and His will. If you desire to activate and engage the ministry of angels, you must first come under the Lordship of Jesus Christ.

Why Does This Matter?

Hebrews 1:14 declares:

"Are not all angels ministering spirits sent to serve those who will inherit salvation?"

To "inherit salvation" means to be a child of God — redeemed, reconciled, and restored to the Father through Jesus

Christ. Angels are not at our beck and call simply because we desire supernatural help. They operate under divine order, responding to those aligned with the will of God.

If you have not yet accepted Jesus Christ as your Lord and Savior, now is the perfect opportunity. The Lord desires to bring you into His family, to secure your eternity, and to position you to experience the fullness of His resources — including the ministry of angels.

A Prayer of Salvation

If you would like to make Jesus the Lord of your life, say this sincerely from your heart:

"Lord Jesus, I acknowledge that I need You. I believe that You died for my sins and rose again to give me eternal life. Today, I repent of my sins, and I invite You to be my Savior and Lord. Fill me with Your Holy Spirit, and help me live a life that pleases You. I receive Your grace, forgiveness, and salvation. In Your name, Jesus, I pray. Amen."

If you prayed this prayer sincerely, welcome to the family of God! You are now an heir of salvation, and the angels are assigned to minister to you (Hebrews 1:14). You have divine authority to speak God's Word, activate angelic help, and live victoriously.

Send an email with **"Newly Saved"** as the subject to hello@gloem.org and we will send you a free resource to help you grow and fully understand your place and authority in Christ Jesus.

40 Angel Activation Prompts: Scriptural Words to Engage Angelic Ministry

Below are 40 carefully curated, biblically grounded prompts you can use to activate angelic ministry effectively. Speak them boldly, in faith, and with the awareness of your identity in Christ.

Protection and Deliverance:

1. *"Angels of the Lord, encamp around me and deliver me from every danger."* (Psalm 34:7)
2. *"Angels assigned to guard me, watch over my home and shield us from all harm."* (Psalm 91:11)
3. *"Ministering spirits, intercept every plot of the enemy set against my life."* (Isaiah 54:17)
4. *"Angels of deliverance, make a way of escape in every crisis I face."* (1 Corinthians 10:13)
5. *"Angels of safety, surround my loved ones in all their going out and coming in."* (Psalm 121:8)

Guidance and Direction:

1. *"Angels of wisdom, go ahead of me and lead me to divine opportunities."* (Psalm 32:8)
2. *"Angels assigned to my destiny, remove every distraction and hindrance to my purpose."* (Hebrews 12:1)
3. *"Ministering spirits, align me with divine connections that will propel my calling."* (Proverbs 3:5-6)

4. *"Angels of revelation, illuminate my understanding in times of decision-making."* (Ephesians 1:17)
5. *"Angels assigned to my path, keep my feet from stumbling into error."* (Psalm 119:105)

Provision and Abundance:

1. *"Angels of provision, bring resources to fulfill God's assignments for my life."* (Philippians 4:19)
2. *"Ministering spirits, connect me with those whose hearts God has touched to support my vision."* (Luke 6:38)
3. *"Angels of breakthrough, open financial doors that no man can shut."* (Revelation 3:8)
4. *"Angels of harvest, gather the fruit of every seed I have sown in faith."* (Galatians 6:9)
5. *"Angels of abundance, cancel every assignment of lack and insufficiency."* (Psalm 23:1)

Healing and Restoration:

1. *"Angels of healing, minister strength and recovery to my body."* (Psalm 107:20)
2. *"Ministering spirits, administer God's power to every area of my life that is broken or wounded."* (Isaiah 53:5)
3. *"Angels assigned to my health, drive out every spirit of infirmity and weakness."* (Matthew 8:16)
4. *"Angels of restoration, release divine health over me and my household."* (Jeremiah 30:17)

5. *"Angels of renewal, revitalize my mind, body, and spirit with God's strength."* (Isaiah 40:31)

Victory in Spiritual Warfare:

1. *"Angels of war, contend with those who contend against me."* (Psalm 35:1)
2. *"Ministering spirits, dismantle every demonic network assigned against my purpose."* (2 Corinthians 10:4)
3. *"Angels of defense, shield me from every fiery dart of the enemy."* (Ephesians 6:16)
4. *"Angels of triumph, enforce the victory Christ won for me on the cross."* (Colossians 2:15)
5. *"Angels of strategy, expose and overturn every scheme of darkness."* (2 Kings 6:17)

Peace and Comfort:

1. *"Angels of peace, calm every storm and silence every chaos in my life."* (Philippians 4:7)
2. *"Ministering spirits, bring comfort to my heart in seasons of grief and loss."* (2 Corinthians 1:3-4)
3. *"Angels assigned to my peace, drive out fear, anxiety, and worry."* (2 Timothy 1:7)
4. *"Angels of rest, release a deep, restorative peace upon my mind and heart."* (Matthew 11:28)
5. *"Ministering spirits, saturate my environment with the peace of God that surpasses understanding."* (Isaiah 26:3)

Activating Angelic Assistance for Others:

1. *"Angels, minister to my family and draw them closer to Christ."* (Acts 16:31)
2. *"Ministering spirits, protect my loved ones from harm and evil influences."* (Psalm 121:7)
3. *"Angels of grace, minister encouragement to those facing difficult seasons."* (Hebrews 1:14)
4. *"Angels of reconciliation, bring healing to broken relationships in my family."* (2 Corinthians 5:18)
5. *"Angels of salvation, help me share the gospel effectively."* (Hebrews 1:14)

Angels and Worship:

1. *"Angels of worship, join me as I magnify God in spirit and truth."* (Hebrews 12:22)
2. *"Angels of adoration, surround my worship with heavenly atmosphere."* (Revelation 5:11-12)
3. *"Ministering spirits, bring God's glory to every place of worship I step into."* (Psalm 22:3)
4. *"Angels of praise, assist me in exalting the Lord with all that I am."* (Psalm 103:20)
5. *"Angels of holiness, reinforce my pursuit of a life pleasing to God."* (1 Peter 1:16)

Contact Us

If you need more information on this subject matter or desire further guidance on walking in the fullness of God's provision through the ministry of angels, feel free to visit www.gloem.org or contact us at hello@gloem.org. We are here to support you in your spiritual journey.

Other Books by the Author: Anthony Adefarakan

It's Your Size

The Immutability of God's Counsel

Surely There Is An End

Learning From the Ants

The Law of Kinds

Life Applicable Lessons from the Book of Ruth

21 Life Applicable Revelations from God's Word Vol.1

21 Life Applicable Revelations from God's Word Vol.2

One Thing is Needful Weekly Devotional Guide

15 Basic Biblical Keys to Poverty

14 Scriptural Principles for Daily Living Vol. 1

14 Scriptural Principles for Daily Living Vol. 2

14 Scriptural Principles for Daily Living Vol. 3

14 Scriptural Principles for Daily Living Vol. 4

14 Scriptural Principles for Daily Living Vol. 5

14 Scriptural Principles for Daily Living Vol. 6

14 Scriptural Principles for Daily Living Vol. 7

Operating the Spirit of Prayer

21 Attributes that God Will Reward

The "LET" Series

GLOEM Gospel Hymnal

Check these titles out and get copies @ https://gloem-tv-shop.fourthwall.com/en-usd or send an email to hello@gloem.org to place orders.

About the Author

Anthony Adefarakan is a renowned revivalist, teacher, evangelist, and visionary leader committed to liberating individuals through the knowledge of the truth of Jesus Christ. He is the Founder and President of Global Emancipation Ministries - Calgary (GLOEM), a global Christian movement with operations spanning Canada, Africa, and beyond. His mission is to empower believers to walk in spiritual and physical emancipation, fulfilling the divine mandate to "liberate people through the knowledge of the Truth" (Isaiah 61:1-3, John 8:32, 36).

Having encountered the Lord at a young age and experienced a powerful restoration in 2002, Anthony fully embraced God's call to ministry in 2008. In 2012, he founded GLOEM, carrying this mission to prisons, hospitals, and underprivileged communities, bringing hope, healing, and supernatural breakthroughs to countless lives.

As a pioneering voice in faith and technology, Anthony is at the forefront of AI-powered Gospel initiatives, digital evangelism, and the intersection of supernatural ministry and technological innovation. His groundbreaking work explores how biblical principles—like those that activate angelic ministry—can align with AI-simulated prompt engineering, unlocking divine intervention with precision and power.

A prolific author and speaker, Anthony has written 29 books, using every available platform—social media, podcasts, print media, and live events—to equip believers to live in freedom, healing, and empowerment through Christ. His messages transcend borders, inspiring a new generation to embrace both the supernatural and strategic advancements for Kingdom impact.

At GLOEM, Jesus is the message, and freedom is the outcome.

Stay Connected:
Website:

www.gloem.org

Social Media:

https://x.com/t4tonyy

https://www.facebook.com/gloem.org

https://www.youtube.com/@GLOEMTV

https://www.linkedin.com/company/global-emancipation-ministries-calgary-canada

https://www.instagram.com/gloemtv/#

https://www.tiktok.com/@gloemtv